the drawings of degas

Introduction by

STEPHEN LONGSTREET

BORDEN PUBLISHING COMPANY

LOS ANGELES

EDGAR HILAIRE GERMAIN DEGAS

1834-1917

He was the most ill-mannered, bitter, introspective and witty of all the Impressionists. He was the only one who ever worked and painted in America, for his mother belonged to the Musson family, long settled in New Orleans. He was born on a June day in 1834 on the Rue St. George, the family name being de Gas. The artist changed it to Degas, dropping the nobiliary particle, and, detesting the name Edgar, always signed his drawings and paintings a simple DEGAS. The family had money, and after studying law, Degas changed his mind and entered the Ecole des Beaux Arts in 1855, thus avoiding the lackadaisical grotesque habits of most art students.

Already a draughtsman of surprising skill, he was wary of friendships, remaining defiant and sardonic. He studied with a pupil of the great Ingres, mastering a style of drawing he worshipped all his life. Degas went to Italy, did hundreds of drawings, copied the precise crisp lines of the 14th century masters, and fell more and more under the classic perfection of Ingres' drawings, and the idea that the only good sin is pride.

In Paris he went through a nearly sterile period of painting great classical oils on legendary or historic subjects, which did not, however, hide his great ability as a draughtsman. The individual drawings he prepared for these pictures are among his early best. Insight and perception blended with a perpetual expenditure of energy.

In 1865 came a great change. Secretive, suffering some inner malaise, playing the loner, Degas broke with his past and changed not only his subject matter but his style. Gone were the classical historic illustrations. Now his drawings in pencil and chalk, in pastels took on horse races, fashionable crowds, cafe scenes and the first of the endless rows of ballet girls, all done with firm vigor and a strong searching line from which nothing vital is ever hidden. One force was the discovery of Japanese prints and the powerful line of Hokusai—a heightened human perception—by the artist who had signed himself: Old-Man-Mad-About-Drawing. Now Degas' work took on almost the casual look of a camera catching the world off guard, candid shots of the people of the *haut monde*, the slaving laundry workers, the sweating overworked ballet girls called 'rats'. Yet it was endowed with the sensibility of lost lives, the haunting mood of irremediable destinies.

To complete the change Degas came to the United States in 1872, to visit a New Orleans uncle and his brothers, Achille and Rene, who were wealthy cotton merchants. Here he painted the only early Impressionist painting done in the United States; his *Cotton Buyer's Office* is a miracle of skill and textures.

He wrote of the new world: "The women are almost all pretty...but weakminded." Degas was always to try to keep women at bay in his life, and at times he did not succeed. His close friendships with Mary Cassatt and Suzanne Valadon, mother of Utrillo, (there is the slight chance Degas was the father of this tainted genius) showed that he often growled most at what he secretly respected, if he respected anything. There was something lost inside Degas, to be endured but never explained.

He returned to Paris to continue his life as a citizen of the boulevards, to haunt and draw the opera, the musicians, the open air concerts, the bibulous cafe drinkers, the horses and fashionable crowds at the race tracks, and most of all the bodies of the ballet girls. He drew them as they were backstage; tired, short, ugly with lumpy over-muscled bodies, drooping breasts, worn practice clothes. Also in the glare of the gaslights, transformed for a moment into the magic of grace and myth, and by his skill into some of the most remarkable graphic works of art of the period, scoring his analytic preferences and prejudices into greatness.

Degas was primarily a draughtsman with a fine tangible sense of color. As he developed he dropped away from Impressionism, which he had never fully embraced, to his own facile, skilled style, often touched by a mood of discontent, yet of obstinate simplicity.

Unlike most western artists he disliked the oil medium in art and turned to drawing in pastels for his final manner, bringing pastel drawing up to the level of great works of art in oil. Emotionally he never crossed over to the world of the irrational, the pattern of incongruity and mystification.

His almost cruel penetration of the secret lives of women at their toilet combines a haunting desire to find the hidden roots of drawing, and to prop up one man's pathological fear of women. He made quick sketches, but he also worked long hours over a pose or a special drawing. He would trace and retrace his drawings repeatedly, improving each tracing, simplifying, catching more of the stance and balance he wanted in the final effect, striving for a deceptive immediacy and spontaneity.

His eyesight always troubled Degas, and by 1890 it was beginning to fail. He could see only one part of an object at a time, and he took to drawing in larger and larger forms and looser and looser shapes. In many ways these late works are his most exciting adventurous forms. When he could hardly find the paper and canvas, he went on modeling in clay and wax, transforming his draughtsmanship into objects he could at least feel. There is something of a boil-plagued Job, something of Michelangelo's last years (with a candle stuck into a cardboard hat on his head) in Degas, old and blind, still snarling his bigotry at the world, his cutting wit still sparring with a society that feared and respected him, and yet aware of a timeless fate that disposes of all as if with one blow.

Alone, but for a housekeeper, in a house shrouded in darkness, his drawings, canvasses, statues piled up, Degas lived into the 20th century. When a painting he had once sold for 500 francs was re-sold for 400,000, he said, "I am like the horse who, having won the Grand Prix, is rewarded by his usual bag of oats."

He rarely went out, but when he did often wrote the hostess a warning: "No flowers on the table, please (he suffered from allergies). Lock up your cat. Be sure no one brings a dog. If there are ladies, will they come undrenched in perfume? What horrors those odors are when one can smell good things like toast...and low and few lights. My eyes, my poor eyes."

The family fortune was gone; he had come upon hard times, but he never descended to any imponderable self pity. Bitter, cynical as he was, in 1914 World War One brought him to the agony of full despair. He sat, blind, in his dusty studio, hearing the guns of the eternal, evil Germans on the Marne. He was eighty; the last of his women-drawings done in rough textured pastels, bathed and scrubbed, their bodies indifferent to the sound of guns and combat. Degas loathed art dealers and critics, he was past caring for the few women he had known. There had been money problems, but all that didn't matter to the sick old man sitting in darkness, listening to his world being knocked to bits. He had rarely let people enter his studio or see him at work. He had remained, he hoped, a gentleman. To the painter Whistler, who had dressed in Bohemian garments, he had said, "You behave as though you had no talent."

He had come, as he said, to the moment "a door shuts inside one...one suppresses everything...I am blocked, impotent...I stored up all my plans in a cupboard...and I have lost the key to it..."

When he was dying in 1917, in the midst of the dreadful war, he told the artist Forain: "No funeral oration for me. If there has to be a word, you get up and just say, 'He greatly loved drawings...'"

STEPHEN LONGSTREET

A Young Woman in Street Costume

Brush drawing with oil, heightened with white

THE FOGG ART MUSEUM, HARVARD UNIVERSITY, CAMBRIDGE, MASS.,
META AND PAUL J. SACHS COLLECTION

The Violinist

Charcoal, heightened with white

MUSEUM OF FINE ARTS, BOSTON, MASS.

Nude Figure Bathing
Charcoal

THE FOGG ART MUSEUM, HARVARD UNIVERSITY, CAMBRIDGE, MASS.,
META AND PAUL J. SACHS COLLECTION

Feminine Nude

Charcoal

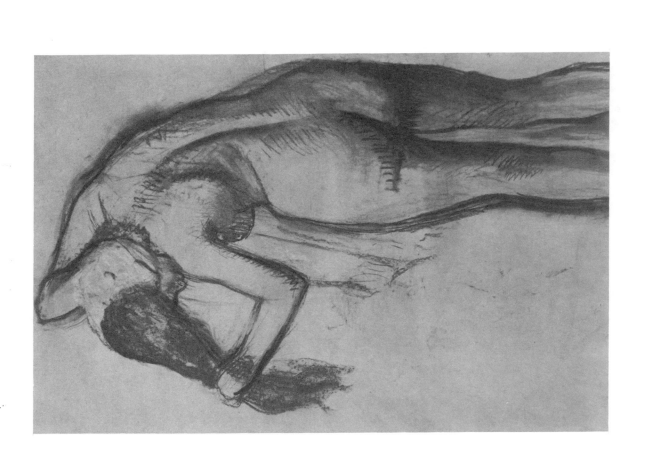

Woman Combing her Hair

Chalk

Dancing Girl with Fan
Black chalk, heightened with white
MUSEUM BOYMANS/VAN BEUNINGEN, ROTTERDAM, HOLLAND

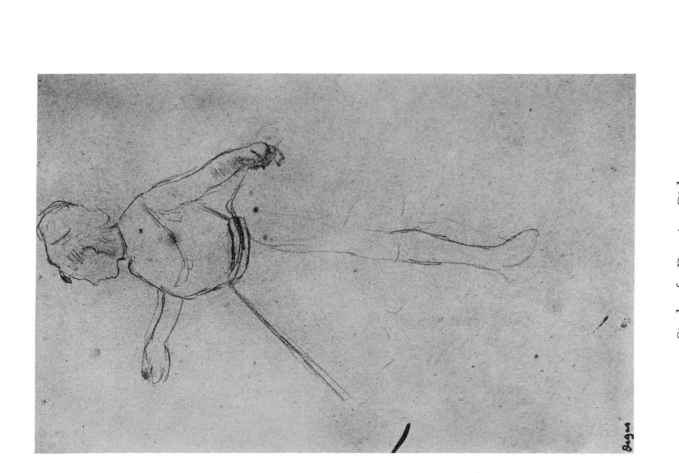

Study of a Dancing Girl
Black chalk on pink paper
MUSEUM BOYMANS/VAN BEUNINGEN, ROTTERDAM, HOLLAND

Figure Study
Pen and ink

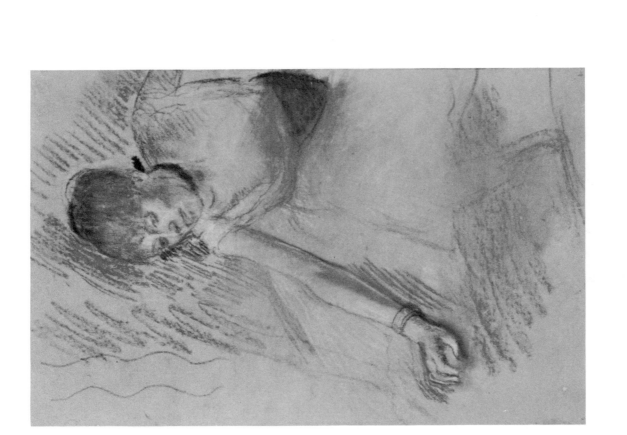

Danseuse
Pastel

Female in Blue

Pastel

THE LOS ANGELES COUNTY MUSEUM, LOS ANGELES, CALIFORNIA
HARRISON COLLECTION

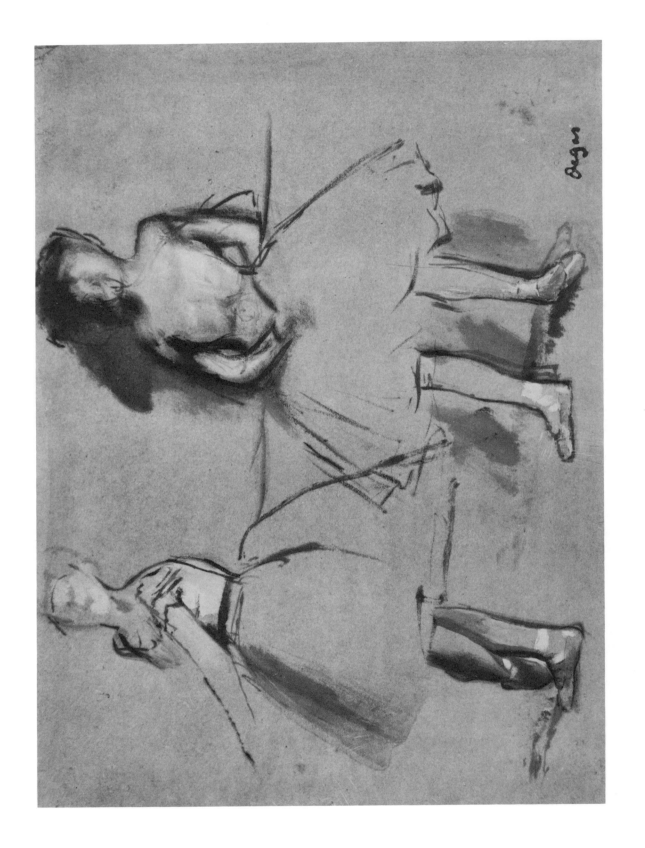

Two Dancing Girls

Brush in brown, white, gray and red, on orange-red paper

MUSEUM BOYMANS/VAN BEUNINGEN, ROTTERDAM, HOLLAND

Study for the Portrait of Diego Martelli

Black crayon, heightened with white

THE FOGG ART MUSEUM, HARVARD UNIVERSITY, CAMBRIDGE, MASS.

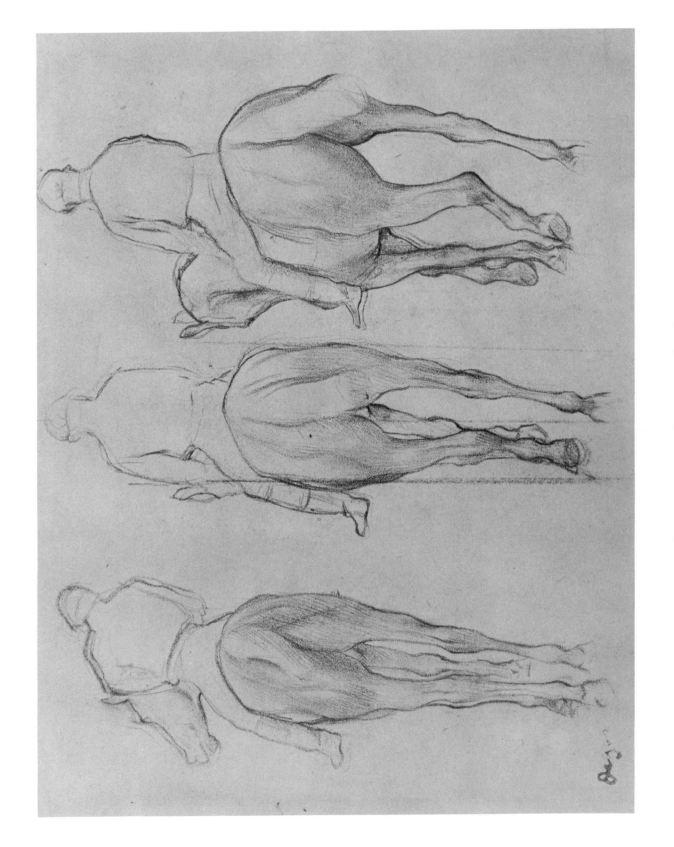

Three Drawings of a Mounted Jockey

Pencil drawing

THE FOGG ART MUSEUM, HARVARD UNIVERSITY, CAMBRIDGE, MASS.

The Duke of Morbilli

Charcoal on white paper

Study for the Portrait of James Tissot

Black crayon

THE FOGG ART MUSEUM, HARVARD UNIVERSITY, CAMBRIDGE, MASS.

GIFT OF C. M. DE KAUKE

Study for the Portrait of Mme. Hertal

Pencil drawing

THE FOGG ART MUSEUM, HARVARD UNIVERSITY, CAMBRIDGE, MASS.
PAUL J. SACHS COLLECTION

Portrait of Edouard Manet

Pen and ink and wash

MME. ERNEST ROUART, PARIS, FRANCE

Nude Figure

Charcoal

After the Bath

Charcoal

THE LOUVRE, PARIS, FRANCE

Danseuse

Pastel

GALERIE ROSENGART, LUCERNE, SWITZERLAND

A Ballet Dancer in Position

Black pencil, heightened with white chalk

THE FOGG ART MUSEUM, HARVARD UNIVERSITY, CAMBRIDGE, MASS.
META AND PAUL J. SACHS COLLECTION

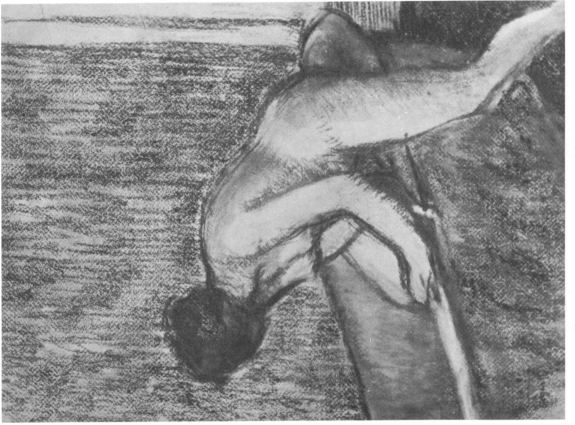

The Bath
Pastel

GALERIE ROSENGART, LUCERNE, SWITZERLAND

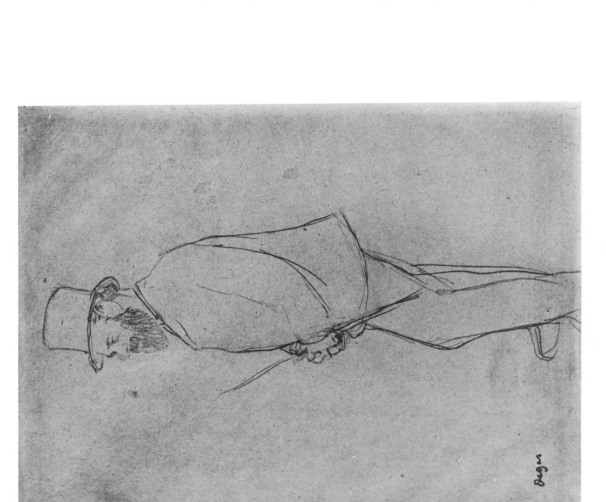

Edouard Manet Standing
Pencil drawing

MUSEUM BOYMANS/VAN BEUNINGEN, ROTTERDAM, HOLLAND

Head of a Horse

Pencil drawing

COURTESY OF THE METROPOLITAN MUSEUM OF ART, NEW YORK CITY, N.Y.
GIFT OF A. E. GALLATIN, 1923

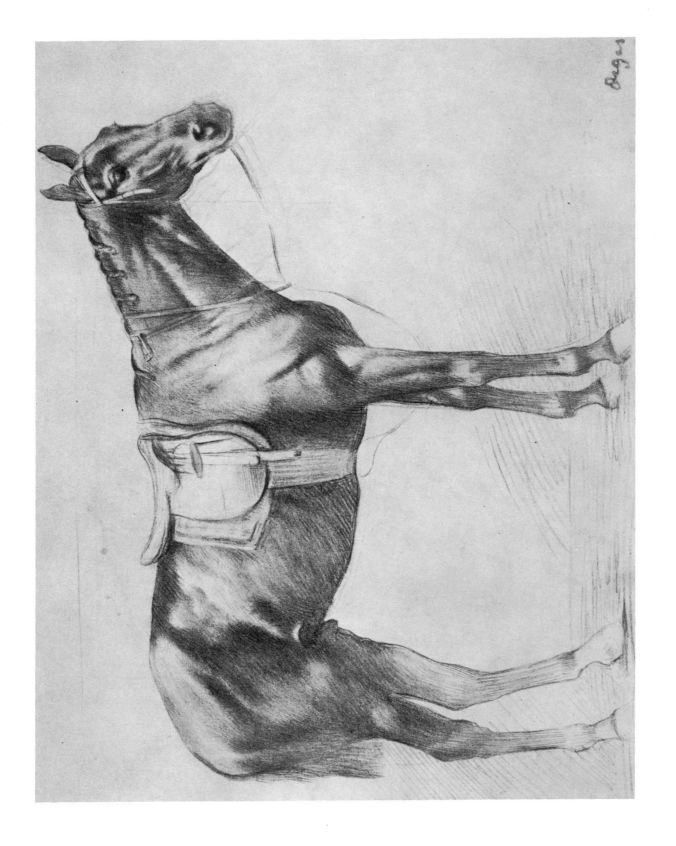

Horse with Saddle and Bridle

Black chalk on buff paper

THE FOGG ART MUSEUM, HARVARD UNIVERSITY, CAMBRIDGE, MASS.

BEQUEST — GRENVILLE L. WINTHROP

Dancer Adjusting Slipper

Pencil and charcoal on pink paper

COURTESY OF THE METROPOLITAN MUSEUM OF ART, NEW YORK CITY, N.Y.
BEQUEST OF MRS. H. O. HAVEMEYER, 1929

Josephine Gaujelin
Pencil drawing

Study of a Dancer
Brown chalk on white paper

Study for the Portrait of Mme. Julie Burtin

Pencil drawing

THE FOGG ART MUSEUM, HARVARD UNIVERSITY, CAMBRIDGE, MASS.

LOAN — PAUL J. SACHS

Study of a Nude Figure

Charcoal and pastel

COURTESY OF THE METROPOLITAN MUSEUM OF ART, NEW YORK CITY, N.Y.,
ROGER FUND, 1918

The Duchess of Morbilli

Charcoal on light brown paper

MUSEUM OF FINE ARTS, BOSTON, MASS.

Russian Dancer

Pastel

COURTESY OF THE METROPOLITAN MUSEUM OF ART, NEW YORK CITY, N.Y.
BEQUEST OF MRS. H. O. HAVEMEYER, 1929

After the Bath

Charcoal on pink paper

THE FOGG ART MUSEUM, HARVARD UNIVERSITY, CAMBRIDGE, MASS.

META AND PAUL J. SACHS COLLECTION

Self Portrait of Edgar Degas
Pen and ink and charcoal
THE LOUVRE, PARIS, FRANCE

Four Studies of a Jockey

Brush with oil

Mademoiselle Dubourg

Black chalk

MUSEUM BOYMANS/VAN BEUNINGEN, ROTTERDAM, HOLLAND

Female Bathing

Charcoal

MUSEUM BOYMANS/VAN BEUNINGEN, ROTTERDAM, HOLLAND

After the Bath

Charcoal

THE FOGG ART MUSEUM, HARVARD UNIVERSITY, CAMBRIDGE, MASS.
META AND PAUL J. SACHS COLLECTION

Self Portrait of Edgar Degas

Red chalk on yellowish paper

COLLECTION OF JOHN NICHOLAS BROWN, PROVIDENCE, R. I.

Little Girl Practicing at the Bar

Charcoal and white chalk

COURTESY OF THE METROPOLITAN MUSEUM OF ART, NEW YORK CITY, N.Y.
BEQUEST OF MRS. H. O. HAVEMEYER, 1929

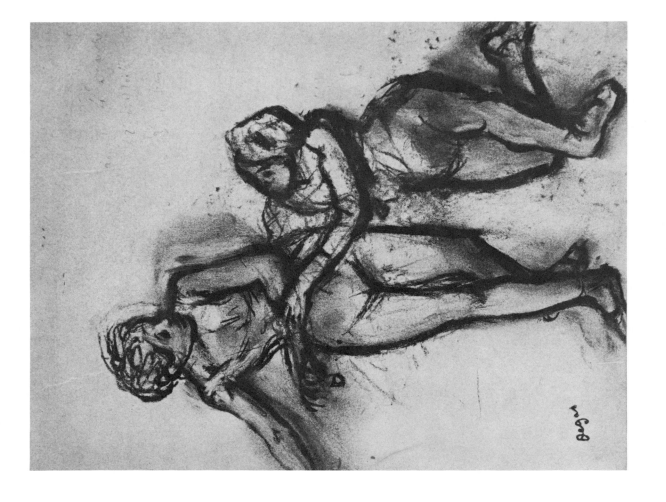

Composition of Two Figures

Charcoal on yellow paper

MUSEUM BOYMANS/VAN BEUNINGEN, ROTTERDAM, HOLLAND

Portrait of Madame Dembrowski

Chalk

MUSEUM BOYMANS/VAN BEUNINGEN, ROTTERDAM, HOLLAND

Study for Portrait of Edouard Manet
Pencil drawing
COURTESY OF THE METROPOLITAN MUSEUM OF ART, NEW YORK CITY, N.Y.
ROGER FUND, 1918

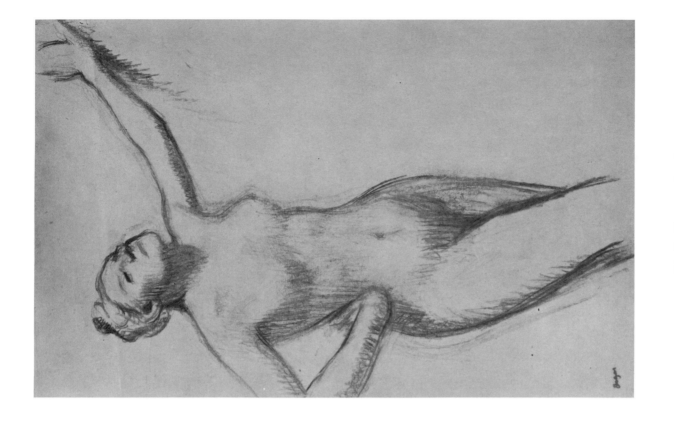

Nude Figure Study
Charcoal

COLLECTION OF J. K. THANNHAUSER, NEW YORK CITY, NEW YORK

Woman with Uplifted Arm
Black chalk on white paper

MUSEUM BOYMANS/VAN BEUNINGEN, ROTTERDAM, HOLLAND

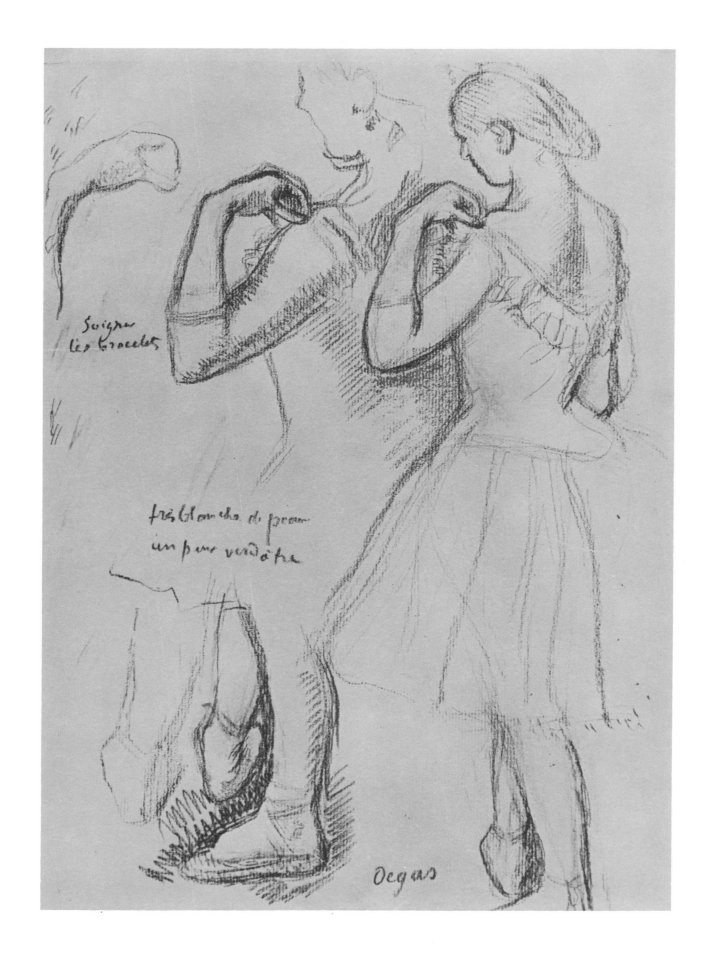

Studies of Dancers

Black crayon

MUSEUM OF FINE ARTS, BUDAPEST, HUNGARY

Dancer and Leg Studies
Pastel drawing

Horse Study
Pencil on grayish Japanese paper

MUSEUM BOYMANS/VAN BEUNINGEN, ROTTERDAM, HOLLAND

Two Women
Black charcoal on white paper
MUSEUM BOYMANS/VAN BEUNINGEN, ROTTERDAM, HOLLAND

Therese Degas, Duchess of Morbilli
Red chalk, heightened with pen in black and washed
MUSEUM BOYMANS/VAN BEUNINGEN, ROTTERDAM, HOLLAND

Dancers

Charcoal drawing

IN THE BROOKLYN MUSEUM COLLECTION, BROOKLYN, NEW YORK

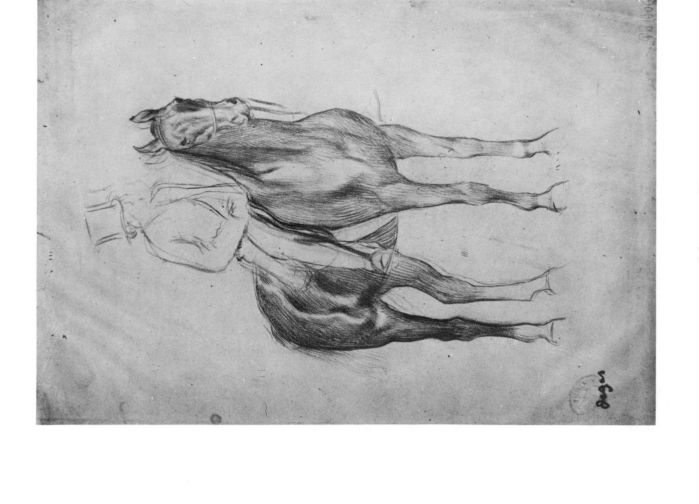

Man on a Horse
Black chalk on white paper

MUSEUM BOYMANS/VAN BEUNINGEN, ROTTERDAM, HOLLAND

Study of Six Heads
Black chalk on white paper

MUSEUM BOYMANS/VAN BEUNINGEN, ROTTERDAM, HOLLAND

Male Nude on Horseback
Charcoal on white paper
MUSEUM BOYMANS/VAN BEUNINGEN, ROTTERDAM, HOLLAND

Study of a Nude Figure
Charcoal and pastel

COURTESY OF THE METROPOLITAN MUSEUM OF ART, NEW YORK CITY, N.Y.
ROGER FUND 1918